A Survival Guide for Parents Part 1

by Dr. John Chanaca

*Nurturing Super Students
in the Modern World"
Part 1*

Published by MJChanacapublishing
Text Copyright 2023
A Survival Guide for Parents
Part 1

www.mjchanacapublishing.com

ISBN-13: 979-8987851074
Paperback
Printed in the USA

"The longer I live, the more I realize the impact of attitude on life. Attitude, to me, is more important than facts. It is more important than the past, than education, than money, than circumstances, than failures, than successes, than what other people think or say or do. It is more important than appearance, giftedness or skill. It will make or break a company...a church....a home. The remarkable thing is we have a choice every day regarding the attitude we will embrace for that day. We cannot change our past...we cannot change the fact that people will act in a certain way. We cannot change the inevitable. The only thing we can do is play on the one string we have, and that is our attitude...I am convinced that life is 10% what happens to me and 90% how I react to it. And so it is with you...we are in charge of our attitudes."
—Charles Swindoll

Acknowledgments

I would like to express my gratitude to all the many people who talked things over, read, wrote, and offered comments.

I need to acknowledge Dr. Robert Bowman, and Susan Bowman, his lovely wife, at YougthLight Inc. and Marco Publishing, who published the <u>original Super Student Program</u> which I authored in 2005.

I want to thank my wife Jane who is my critic and best friend. Also, a special thanks to my brother and master teacher, David who is always encouraging and faithful with great suggestions.

Thanks to my children and grandchildren who have supported me in this retirement era to start a publishing company that produces wholesome books for young people.

Last but not least, I want to thank my God for bringing to me wonderful teachers and people who would direct my work and my life.

Part 1

Any program in American education would only be complete with parental involvement. Parents are vital as partners and need to feel and know that they are the primary influence in helping their children become Super Students.

You are your children's first and best teacher!

What we want our children to do:

- Take responsibility for their learning

- Learn a systematic model for improving their schoolwork

- Improve effort toward academic tasks

- Absorb basic study skills and concepts that improve the effectiveness and efficiency of their learning

- Enhance self-esteem in the learning experience

- Develop as lifelong learners with positive, healthy attitudes

Introduction

As parents or grandparents, you are not only the first but also the best teachers for your children. Good parenting has always been paramount in raising well-rounded individuals. However, in our current times, parenting has become increasingly challenging. Today's parents face unprecedented pressures and strains as they strive to nurture positive, healthy, happy, and educated young minds. The complexities of modern life, including marital problems, economic concerns, the prevalence of drugs, sexual challenges, the alarming rise in mass shootings, pervasive media influence, and the relentless peer pressures, are just a few of the formidable obstacles that parents and grandparents encounter as they endeavor to raise disciplined self-learners.

Amid these trials and tribulations, it is crucial to acknowledge that no one else possesses such a significant impact on your child's life as you do. You hold the key to unlocking their potential and shaping their future.

1. How do you create an environment that fosters a love for learning and encourages your child to become a diligent student?

2. How can you actively contribute to your child's development as a lifelong learner?

These are the questions we will explore together. In the following sections, we will delve into practical strategies and effective approaches to empower you to cultivate Super Student concepts and skills within your children.

Let's Begin

Parental involvement is not only a responsibility; it is an opportunity to guide, inspire, and ignite the spark of curiosity and passion for knowledge within your child. By actively engaging in their educational journey, you can help them build a strong foundation for success, both academically and personally.

Section 1: Building Belief in Oneself and Essential Skills for Lifelong Learning

1. Believe in yourself as an effective parent so that your child can flourish as a student. You demonstrate faith in your abilities by creating an environment that nurtures your child's growth and development.

2. Know that God loves you and has a plan for your life. You must understand that you are destined and designed to guide your child and that your role as a parent is purposeful.

3. Know that you have been chosen to embark on this incredible journey of parenthood. Each child is a precious gift. Embrace this truth with conviction, knowing you have a significant role in shaping their future.

4. Instill a lifelong love for learning in your child by demonstrating an unwavering belief in their potential. Let them know, time and again, that you have absolute confidence in their abilities.

5. Cultivate a positive attitude, both within yourself and your child. Belief and attitude are the driving forces behind their success. By fostering a mindset of optimism, perseverance, and self-belief, you empower your child to overcome challenges and reach their full academic potential.

6. **Being loving, respectful, hard-working, obedient, trusting, and kind are the skills that set the foundation for success in school and beyond.** While not everyone may need to become a doctor, lawyer, or engineer, we must embrace these moral and ethical qualities.

7. **Being a good student is about more than just academic achievements.** It is about developing core values and character traits that lead to success in all aspects of life.

8. **By consciously or subconsciously embodying the following focus skills, students thrive academically.** They become compassionate individuals who know how to thrive in school and contribute positively to society.

Section 2: Focus Skills for Super Students

When helping your child become a Super Student, it's essential to focus on specific skills that will enhance their learning experience and contribute to their overall success in the classroom. Here are eight critical focus skills that you can teach your children:

1. I will listen, obey, and trust my teacher: Encourage your child to actively listen to their teacher, follow instructions, and trust in their guidance. This skill helps create a positive and cooperative classroom environment.

2. I will raise my hand to speak: Teach your child the importance of raising their hand and waiting for their turn to speak. This skill fosters respectful communication and allows everyone to be heard.

3. I will think along with the speaker: Encourage your child to actively engage their minds while listening to the teacher or their peers. Encouraging critical thinking and active participation helps develop their cognitive abilities.

4. I will be prepared for my work: Instill in your child the habit of preparing for each class by completing assignments and bringing the necessary materials. Being organized and ready promotes productivity and ensures they can fully participate in classroom activities.

5. I will give my best: Emphasize the importance of putting forth their best effort in all tasks and assignments. Please encourage them to take pride in their work and strive for personal excellence.

6. I will finish all my work: Teach your child the value of perseverance and completing tasks. Emphasize the importance of seeing tasks through to the end and avoiding procrastination.

7. I will work out problems with others: Foster a collaborative mindset by teaching your child the importance of working together with their classmates to solve problems. Encourage effective communication, teamwork, and empathy.

8. I will have a positive, healthy attitude: Help your child develop a positive mindset and attitude toward learning. Teach them resilience, optimism, and the importance of maintaining a healthy emotional state.

Summary

1.To effectively teach these focus skills, discuss each with your child and discuss their significance. Then, please encourage your child to practice these skills daily in the classroom and observe their progress.

2. You can also use these focus skills as a checklist during meetings with your child's teacher to assess their development. By incorporating these skills into their daily routine, your child will naturally engage in the learning process, and academic achievement will follow.

3. Learning is a natural process. When these focus skills are embraced, the love for learning and academic growth will naturally occur.

4. In addition, by nurturing these focus skills, you empower your child to become self-directed learners. This sets the stage for lifelong success in their academic and personal endeavors.

Section 3: The Importance of Listening, Obeying, and Trusting the Teacher

Listening to, obeying, and trusting the teacher is the first crucial focus skill, forming the foundation for a student's success in the classroom. It serves as the cornerstone upon which all other focus skills are built.

1. **Support your child's teacher by attending all conferences and meetings.** By actively engaging in these interactions, you demonstrate your commitment to your child's education and build a partnership with the teacher.

2. **Take the time to get to know your child's teacher as a person and understand their teaching methods.** This open line of communication will foster a sense of trust and cooperation.

3. Let your child know that you support the teacher and recognize their authority. Insist that your child respects their teacher. Establish an atmosphere where respect for authority is expected. You set a positive example for your child by modeling respect for the teacher.
When you question or challenge the teacher's decisions in front of your child, it sends a message that it is acceptable to be disrespectful and disobedient.

5. This act undermines your child's ability to listen, obey, and trust their teacher. To avoid this, if you disagree with a teacher, address it privately between you and the teacher.

6. Seek to work out any differences through respectful dialogue. You can refer the matter to the principal or administration if a resolution is impossible. However, it is crucial to handle these discussions discreetly without discussing the negative aspects of the teacher in front of your child. If communication is impossible, change the teacher or the school.

7. As a parent, supporting your child in school profoundly demonstrates love. As a result, you can help them develop into healthy and well-rounded individuals. In addition, it is a chance for both you and your child to grow and learn together.

8. Your behavior is a model for your child. Being the best version of yourself is essential. Embodying values such as honesty, respect, strong work ethic, goodness, and love will give your child values to emulate.

Summary

Giving your child support during their school years is one of the most important things you can do for them to show your love. They are only young once. You can help them develop into healthy young adults. Then, as a bonus, you grow along the way!

How is this possible? God has given us a chance to grow up twice. Because your child models your behavior, you need to be all you can be so your child can see what honesty, respect, work ethic, goodness, and love are.

Remember, your role as a parent extends beyond supporting your child academically. You must also nurture their overall growth and well-being.

By fostering a positive relationship with your child's teacher and demonstrating respect for authority, you create an environment that encourages your child to listen, obey, and trust their teacher.

Please look at these Focus Skills to help your child become a Super Student in class.

1. I will listen, obey, and trust my teacher.

2. I will raise my hand to speak.

3. I will think along with the speaker.

4. I will be prepared with my work.

5. I will give my best.

6. I will finish all my work.

7. I will work out problems with others.

8. I will have a positive, healthy attitude.

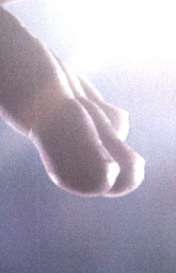

The End

Of the Beginning

Thank you for Reading

"A Survival Guide for Parents Part 1 "

a three part series.

In Part 2, we will explore some parenting skills that promote a positive and loving attitude that will make your child a winner in school and life.

Please leave your email at www.mjchanacapublishing.com

A Word From
the Author

This book is a guide. Every family is different. These suggestions must be adapted into a family according to the individual situations that exist. I believe we live in a world that is in a constant spiritual battle between good and evil. We, as parents, have to make choices. As Charles Swindoll said in the opening quote of this book, "The remarkable thing is we have a choice every day regarding the attitude we will embrace for that day." God helps us to make these choices for good. I have also put together books for students in the elementary and middle grades to help with these skills. "The Keymaker" is the first in this series with others to follow.   John

About the Author

Dr. John Chanaca has over 42 years of teaching/counseling experience in PA and SC public schools. After completing his bachelor's and master's degrees in elementary education, he taught in various elementary and middle schools at multiple locations with different socioeconomic and cultural groups. He obtained his certification in counseling from Marywood University in PA. John also holds a certificate in public School administration from Penn State University. In addition, he has been a Licensed Professional Counselor (LPC) since 1985 and has a private Christian Marriage and Family Practice.

John received his Doctorate in Education from the University of South Carolina (1992), concentrating in curriculum and instruction.

In October of 1998, Dr. Chanaca was selected as a Fulbright Memorial Fund Scholar to Japan to study their educational system. This trip inspired Dr. Chanaca to begin writing the Super Student Program published by Youghtlight, Inc. This program was designed to improve, recognize and celebrate student achievement and behavior.

He is a co-author of the AGS program Peer Pals. This program has received several national and state awards. Peers Pals is a motivational program for elementary school students focusing on positive learning attitudes and self-esteem in peer-helping situations.

Dr. Chanaca is a third-degree Black Belt in Tang Soo Do martial arts. He was the owner and head instructor of Live Oaks Academy for over 17 years, producing over 25 Black Belt instructors.

He has taught Adult Sunday School for over 30 years and is currently involved in The English Cafe, a lay Christian missionary program sharing the Christian Gospel via Zoom worldwide.
He can be found at www.mjchanacapublishing.com

MJChanacapublishing is a family values-oriented publishing company. We publish heartwarming stories that reach out to individuals and family members to educate, entertain, and share positive values. The stories are wholesome and often teach moral and ethical values. Stay in touch if you are interested in this type of reading because we have seven books ready to go in 2023. They will be published in paperback, hardcover, e-book, and audible formats. Stay tuned. John, Jane, and The Team.

Find us at www.mjchanacapublishing.com

"Finally, brothers and sisters, whatever is true, whatever is noble, whatever is right, whatever is pure, whatever is lovely, whatever is admirable-if anything is excellent or praiseworthy-think about such things."
Philippians 4:8 NIV

Unleash the Magic of Lacor: "The Keymaker"

Step into the captivating realm of Lacor, where curiosity and courage ignite the spirits of two young students on an extraordinary adventure with their eagle friend, Talon! Brace yourself for a thrilling journey that will test their resolve and determination. Are they prepared to confront the ultimate battle between light and darkness? The choice is theirs to make!

In this enchanting children's book, prepare to be transported to a world brimming with wonder and enchantment. As our young heroes try to find their way to the Keymaker, they encounter challenges that will try their will and determination to the limit. But fear not! Their mentor, the Keymaker, a wise, elderly friend, will light their path, offering sage advice and leading them toward their destiny.

"The Keymaker" is an exhilarating and thought-provoking tale that will captivate young minds and hearts alike. It delves into the profound value of choice and presents the mysteries of Lacor, where the forces of good and evil clash in a battle of epic proportions for students.

Prepare to be swept away by the sheer magic and intrigue of this book for young people.

MJ Chanaca publishing **Super Student Series** **MJ** Chanaca publishing

The Super Student Series is devoted to improving student behavior and academic achievement. The books in this series challenge students to be personally responsible for their learning by giving them the survival tools necessary to win in school today. Through engaging, entertaining adventure and action stories, this series encourages students to be winners in school and teaches them the secrets of success.

We are excited about our recently published book, "The Keymaker," the first book in our "Super Student Series." And now, "A Survival Guide for Parents Part 1" is available on Amazon. Part 2 is coming soon! Dr. John Chanaca, our founder/author, wrote all three of these beautifully illustrated parenting books.

Both are here NOW available in the summer/fall of 2023. On sale now in EBOOK, and PAPERBACK on Amazon! Part 2 is coming soon!

Find both at www.mjchanacapublishing.com

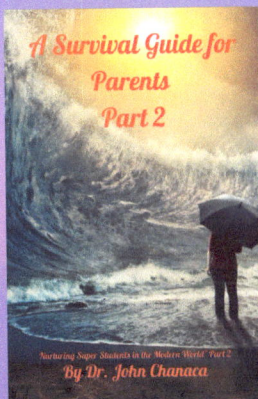

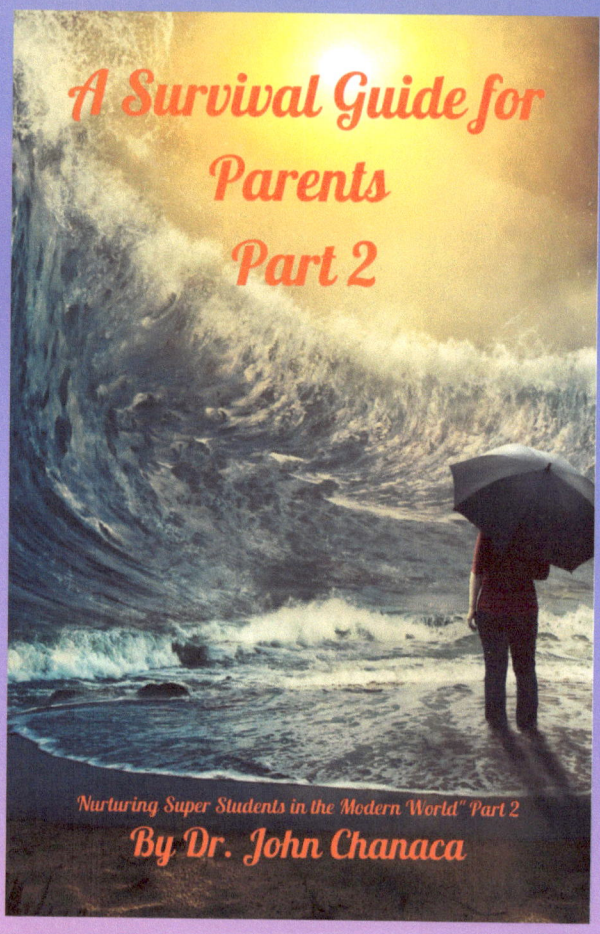

A Survival Guide for Parents Part 2

Nurturing Super Students in the Modern World" Part 2

By Dr. John Chanaca

Receive your Free ebook copy by
giving your email at
www.mjchanacaoublishig.com
until this book is published